Sign Language Man

Gallaudet and His Incredible Work

Edwin Brit Wyckoff

Enslow Elementary

an imprint of

Enslow Publishers, Inc.

40 Industrial Road
Box 398
Berkeley Heights, NJ 07922
USA

http://www.enslow.com

Content Adviser
Catherine C. Valcourt-Pearce
Coordinator, Publications and Development
Laurent Clerc National Deaf Education Center
Gallaudet University

Series Literacy Consultant
Alan A. De Fina, Ph.D.
Dean, College of Education and Professor of Literacy Education
New Jersey City University
Past President, New Jersey Reading Association

Enslow Elementary, an imprint of Enslow Publishers, Inc.

Enslow Elementary® is a registered trademark of Enslow Publishers, Inc.

Library of Congress Cataloging-in-Publication Data

Wyckoff, Edwin Brit.
  Sign language man : Thomas H. Gallaudet and his incredible work / Edwin Brit Wyckoff.
     p. cm. — (Genius at work! Great inventor biographies)
  Includes index.
  Summary: "Read about Thomas H. Gallaudet, who helped develop and teach American Sign Language"—Provided by publisher.
  ISBN 978-0-7660-3447-1
  1. Gallaudet, T. H. (Thomas Hopkins), 1787-1851—Juvenile literature. 2. Teachers of the deaf—United States—Biography—Juvenile literature. 3. American Sign Language—History—Juvenile literature. I. Title.
  HV2534.G3W93 2011
  371.91'2092—dc22
  [B]
                                         2010005359

Printed in the United States of America

072010 Lake Book Manufacturing, Inc., Melrose Park, IL

10 9 8 7 6 5 4 3 2 1

To Our Readers
We have done our best to make sure all Internet Addresses in this book were active and appropriate when we went to press. However, the author and the publisher have no control over and assume no liability for the material available on those Internet sites or on other Web sites they may link to. Any comments or suggestions can be sent by e-mail to comments@enslow.com or to the address on the back cover. Every effort has been made to locate all copyright holders of material used in this book. If any errors or omissions have occurred, corrections will be made in future editions of this book.

♻ Enslow Publishers, Inc., is committed to printing our books on recycled paper. The paper in every book contains 10% to 30% post-consumer waste (PCW). The cover board on the outside of each book contains 100% PCW. Our goal is to do our part to help young people and the environment too!

Photo Credits: Associated Press, pp. 18, 23, 27; Mary Evans Picture Library/The Image Works, p. 12; Gallaudet University Archives, pp. 13, 22; The Granger Collection, New York, pp. 1 (portrait), 20; Library of Congress, pp. 8, 10, 25; Photo Researchers, p. 16; Shutterstock.com, pp. 1, 3, 4, 14, 19, 29; © Michael Ventura/PhotoEdit, p. 26; Wikimedia Commons, p. 6.

Front cover photos: © David Young-Wolff/PhotoEdit (large photo); The Granger Collection, New York (small inset photo).

Back cover photo: Shutterstock.com.

Note: Front cover shows a little girl signing to her baby brother; p. 1 shows the sign for "interpreter"; p. 3 and the back cover show the sign for "I love you."

Contents

Chapter 1

The Glass Jar

Five afternoons a week, big and little dogs trotted over to the school yard. They flopped down comfortably and waited as if they had watches telling them the exact time school was over. With a steely bang the school bell rang. The doors burst open. Girls and boys ran out. Dogs and children raced and chased every which way, shouting, laughing, and shouting again.

One little girl did not. She sat in her garden just watching. It seemed as though she were in a glass jar. She could see out, but she did not seem to hear a single word or even the sound of the biggest dog barking.

A young man watched the little girl who never moved from her front yard. And he wondered about her. He asked one of the boys racing by. The boy shouted out that Alice never spoke. Alice Cogswell could not hear anything—not even her own voice.

The young man strolled over while nine-year-old Alice stared at the children. He tapped her shoulder, and she spun around to see his lips silently say, "My name is Thomas . . . Thomas Hopkins Gallaudet." (His name is pronounced gal-uh-DET.) He picked up a stick and scratched the letters H A T in a patch of dirt. Then he handed her his hat. Nothing happened.

He scratched the letters H A T again and again, handing her his hat each time. Finally she traced H A T with her fingers in the soft earth, then slapped the hat on her head with a smile as big as the sun. She started

Alice Cogswell

tapping her chest harder and harder. She said no words, but Gallaudet knew what she wanted. Together they scratched out the letters A L I C E. She grabbed Gallaudet's hand and dragged him into her house to meet her father, Dr. Mason Cogswell. She scrawled A L I C E on a piece of paper. Then she whirled around and around, hugging herself with joy. It was 1815. Thomas Hopkins Gallaudet and Alice Cogswell were at the beginning of a revolution in teaching the deaf to talk without making a sound.

Chapter 2

Doors Slammed Shut

Wildly happy, Dr. Cogswell called on friends and businessmen from his town of Hartford, Connecticut. He wanted money to start a school for the deaf. And he wanted them to meet twenty-eight-year-old Gallaudet, who, Cogswell thought, would make an excellent teacher.

In many countries, deaf children were left to roam the streets. They were not taught or taken care of. They were "the children of silence" trapped in a very quiet world. In the United States, they were called "deaf and dumb." (*Dumb* did not mean "stupid." It meant "unable to speak.") They were kept at home for safety. They might be taught a trade like leatherwork or weaving or trained to do household work. Almost no

A statue of Gallaudet and Alice

one thought that deaf children could learn to read and write. Gallaudet believed that they could.

Thomas Hopkins Gallaudet was born in Philadelphia, Pennsylvania, on December 10, 1787. He was the first of ten children born to Peter Wallace Gallaudet and Jane Hopkins. The growing family settled in Hartford, Connecticut, in 1800.

Thomas loved to read, but he had weak eyes and difficulty breathing. He knew what it was like seeing others running and playing while he struggled with a constant cough.

The boy's mind was like a magnet for facts and ideas. When he was fifteen, he started classes at Yale College. His test scores were so high that he was able to skip the first year. He got top grades in math, history, Greek, and Latin. Thomas had a talent for turning his ideas into winning arguments. He was elected president of the college debating team. And he graduated with honors in 1805.

Doctors told the skinny young man with the painful, constant cough that he would become stronger and healthier if he spent time working outdoors in the open air. So Gallaudet came up with a bold idea. He packed up saddlebags with pins, needles, knives, pots, and pans and rode his horse through Kentucky and Ohio, selling his goods from town to town. At the end of the season, he returned to Hartford to study law. But the clouds of tobacco smoke swirling through the office air made him sick again.

Thomas Gallaudet returned to college to study religion. He became a minister in 1814, but he had to turn down good job

Gallaudet attended Yale College when he was only fifteen years old.

offers from churches because his eyes and lungs could not stand the strain.

Suddenly everything changed. Alice's father and his friends begged Gallaudet to learn more about teaching the deaf. He could not turn them down. But before he could teach, he had to know more than A L I C E and H A T.

Gallaudet sailed for England on May 25, 1815. The leading English experts on teaching the deaf were a family named Braidwood. They carefully kept their methods secret. They insisted that Gallaudet work for them without pay for three to five years and promise not to share with others what he learned. He turned them down, and the Braidwoods slammed their door in his face. Gallaudet's time and money were running out fast.

Chapter 3

Flying Fingers

Convinced that he had failed, Thomas Gallaudet walked through the rainy, foggy streets of London, England. He spotted a poster advertising a demonstration of French Sign Language. Sad, but still hopeful, he entered the hall where it was being held.

The demonstration was led by a famous French teacher of the deaf, Abbé Roch-Ambroise Cucurron Sicard. (*Abbé,* pronounced "ah-BAY," is the French word for "priest.") Abbé Sicard was onstage with two

Abbé Sicard was a famous French teacher of the deaf.

Jean Massieu and Laurent Clerc were two deaf teachers who worked with Abbé Sicard.

of his deaf students who had become teachers, Jean Massieu and Laurent Clerc. People in the audience asked Abbé Sicard a question. The abbé turned to the two men, who were watching his hands carefully.

Silently, Abbé Sicard used fingerspelling to make letters and handshapes that represented whole words. The question was "What kind of women do you like best?" Laurent Clerc wrote his answer in

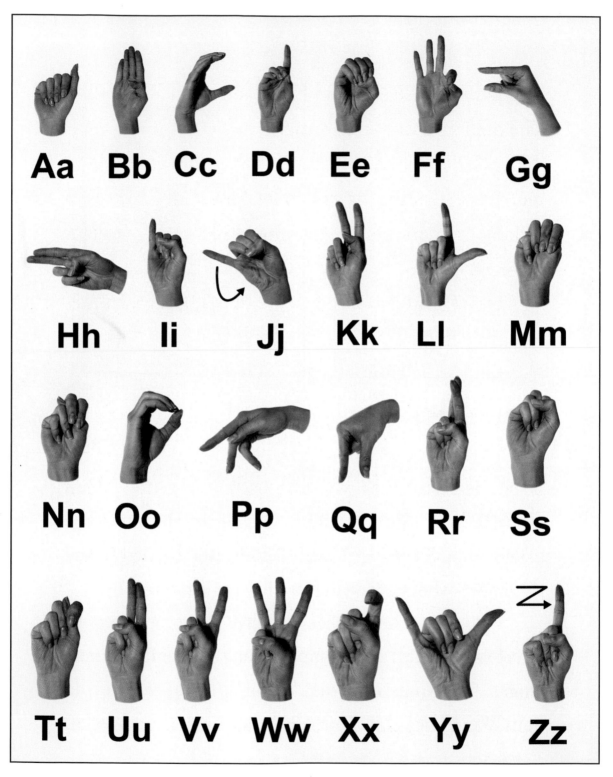

The alphabet in American Sign Language

English on a blackboard: "I like all women equally." The applause was staggering.

Gallaudet asked the Frenchmen to teach him more. Abbé Sicard offered to let him study in France as long as he needed. And it would not cost Gallaudet a penny.

Gallaudet accepted the offer and then asked for a much bigger favor. He wanted Laurent Clerc to work with him in Hartford. On the long voyage to America, Gallaudet would teach Clerc English and the Frenchman would teach him how to use sign language to talk to the deaf. Together they would show America that the deaf could "hear" with their eyes and "speak" with their hands. The generous Abbé Sicard agreed.

It was not easy. In addition to working to develop American Sign Language, with hundreds and then thousands of word signs that would fill a dictionary, they had to work on special grammar that

Genius at Work!

There are finger signs for each letter. But spelling out all the words would take a very long time. So wordshapes signaling whole words and concepts were developed.

The sign for "father"

Five fingers spread apart with the thumb tapping the forehead means FATHER. The same gesture with the thumb tapping the chin means MOTHER. Moving that sign down to tap the chest means FINE. The signs are silent, and the sentences are designed to be understood quickly.

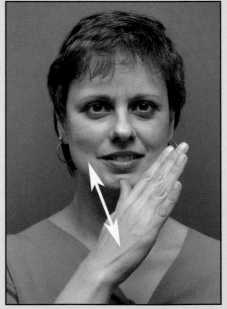

The sign for "mother"

worked naturally for the deaf. Gallaudet and Clerc also spent days, nights, and weekends teaching classes and raising money for a school in Hartford.

Surprisingly, they faced objections from people in America who accused them of playing tricks and cheating. Deafness was a brain defect that could not be cured, people said angrily. Many were convinced that the deaf would never learn to communicate. Crowds actually threw rotten eggs during sign language demonstrations.

Facing them down, Gallaudet had some success in raising money. The Connecticut legislature voted to contribute five thousand dollars. The school's bank account grew to seventeen thousand dollars. A school building was rented. Seven students came to study. Some were almost grown up. Others were as young as Alice Cogswell. They learned to read and write, and they learned American Sign Language—also known as ASL—as fast as it was developed.

Gallaudet and Clerc borrowed some signs that deaf people who lived together had worked out for themselves. They even took some signs that American Indians used for communicating silently as they hunted. The teachers kept on expanding a whole language of signs. The deaf might not hear, but they could talk with their hands, listen with their eyes, and even tell stories in a language that belonged to them.

By 1819 there were 125 students in the school. In 1830, the U.S. Congress gave the school some land. It was more than was needed, so the school sold some

The American School for the Deaf celebrated its 185th anniversary in 2002. The wooden hands spell out "ASD 185" in American Sign Language.

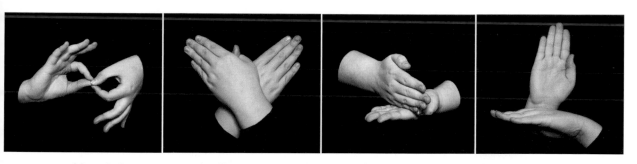

Handshapes can indicate complex words or concepts. Shown above (left to right) are the signs for INTERPRETER, BUTTERFLY, STOP, and BUSY.

of it to get money to construct a new building in Hartford. It was called the Connecticut Asylum for the Education and Instruction of Deaf and Dumb Persons. The name was later changed to the American School for the Deaf. It was the first permanent school for deaf children in America. Gallaudet became the first principal of the new school.

Chapter 4

Hard Times

Gallaudet's workload as principal of the school became overwhelming. He taught six classes a day, gave tours of the school, ordered supplies, found and trained new teachers, wrote schoolbooks, and put together a sign language dictionary with thousands of

A drawing from 1842 shows Gallaudet with some of his students.

signs. And he still traveled to give demonstrations of ASL in other cities.

The school had a board of directors—a group of people in charge of hiring teachers and managing the school. Always under pressure to meet expenses, they became difficult to work for. The board gave pay raises to some teachers, but gave nothing more to Gallaudet. They elected a school president over him. The board acted as though they owned him. They counted on Gallaudet's being too gentle to complain.

Gallaudet found time and courage to propose marriage to

A Separate Language

ASL is not an exact copy of English. It is a separate language. For instance, look at the following sentences in English, then in ASL:

English: We went to the store to buy candy.

ASL: WE STORE GO BUY CANDY.

English: I'm bored. What do you want to do tonight?

ASL: BORED I. DO TONIGHT?

English: Did you see in the paper about an accident on the freeway? I saw it.

ASL: SEE NEWSPAPER FREEWAY ACCIDENT, I SEE IT.

American Sign Language sentences are not strange English. They are absolutely correct grammar in ASL.

This is Sophia Fowler Gallaudet.

one of his first deaf students. The "rare and radiant" Sophia Fowler married him on August 29, 1821. Their first son, Edward, was born in 1822. Eventually, Sophia and Thomas Gallaudet had eight children.

Working for the board of directors got more difficult. They hired a superintendent to run things. They even asked the overworked Gallaudet to resign. But the school's teachers fought back for him. Five of them threatened to resign if Gallaudet left. They called on citizens of Hartford to show up to support their principal. They won, but Gallaudet was worn out by fighting and working for almost nothing except his love of his "children of silence." He resigned as principal in 1830. He had won the war, but could not take the battle any longer.

Chapter 5

"Dream Your Dreams"

Today, ASL is the fourth most used language in America. There are also many sign language interpreters. They listen to a speaker and translate the words into ASL for deaf and hard-of-hearing people, or they translate ASL into English for a

A sign language interpreter translates a speech by President Obama.

23

hearing audience. It is fascinating to see their hands in motion, the face acting out the story, the lips adding to the message, energy pouring out from interpreter to audience. The whole body works to send the message. Interpreters work in classrooms, courtrooms, theaters and churches—anywhere their skills are needed to help people communicate. Gallaudet's work made these things possible.

The weak little boy who found it so hard to breathe had grown up with a will of iron. He fought for the rights of deaf people. In the beginning, he wondered and worried about one little girl named Alice. In the end, he developed and taught a new language that millions would use. And all his life he fought so that deaf people could live better lives.

Gallaudet never stopped developing new signs and better ways to teach the deaf. After he retired, he began writing about education for the deaf and writing books for children. He turned down offers to preach and teach at famous churches and colleges. He became a minister at a jail and at a hospital for mentally ill people. Gallaudet had a gift for reaching people locked away from the world the way Alice Cogswell had been so long ago.

Thomas Gallaudet rarely seemed to be discouraged. When he was tired, his wife comforted him by signing, "DREAM. DREAM YOUR DREAMS OF WHAT MIGHT BE." Gallaudet

Edward Miner Gallaudet founded what became Gallaudet University, the first liberal-arts university for deaf people.

might have dreamed of a great university for the deaf with all classes taught in ASL. He could have dreamed that his son Edward Miner Gallaudet would become the first president of what is now known as Gallaudet University in Washington, D.C. And it may be that his dream university had thousands of deaf

Gallaudet University, the first liberal-arts university specifically for deaf and hard-of-hearing people

students learning to become teachers, scientists, lawyers, accountants, and engineers.

Thomas Hopkins Gallaudet died at home September 10, 1851, saying, "I will go to sleep," as he turned over in bed. And all those dreams came true.

Students using ASL

Timeline

1787   Thomas H. Gallaudet born December 10 in Philadelphia, Pennsylvania, to Peter Wallace Gallaudet and Jane Hopkins.

1800   The Gallaudet family moves to Hartford, Connecticut.

1802   Passes test for Yale University. Skips freshman year. Becomes president of Yale debating team.

1805   Graduates with a bachelor of science degree. Becomes a traveling peddler selling goods in Kentucky and Ohio for a year. Joins a New York firm.

1814   Becomes a minister. Meets Alice Cogswell and her father in Hartford, Connecticut.

1815   Travels to England hoping to study methods of teaching deaf people. Meets French teachers of the deaf Abbé Sicard, Laurent Clerc, and Jean Massieu.

1816   Studies in France. Brings Laurent Clerc back to America with him.

1817   Becomes first principal of the Connecticut Asylum for the Education and Instruction of Deaf and Dumb Persons (now the American School for the Deaf) in Hartford.

1821   Marries Sophia Fowler August 29. They have eight children.

1830   Resigns as school principal to earn money as a writer and raise his large family. Writes many books for children and about teaching the deaf.

1838   Becomes a minister at a hospital for the mentally ill in Hartford.

1851   Dies on September 10.

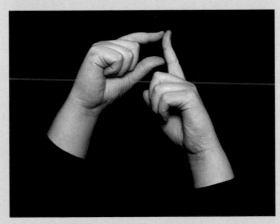

The sign for "word".

Words to Know

American Sign Language (ASL)—A language made up of finger signs for letters and handshapes that illustrate whole words or concepts.

board of directors—A group of people elected to be in charge of an organization.

debating—An activity in which two teams argue different sides of a topic. The arguments are scored to decide the winning team.

interpreter—Someone who watches or listens to a speaker and translates what is said into a language an audience can understand. Interpreters for the deaf use sign language to get the message across.

radiant—Glowing with beauty.

resign (ree-ZINE)—To quit a job.

translate—To turn one language into another language. Interpreters listen to English and translate it into ASL, or they watch ASL and translate it into English.

university—A college that has specialized schools in such subjects as law, medicine, or education. Harvard, Howard, Yale, and Gallaudet are universities.

Books

Heller, Lora. *Sign Language for Kids: A Fun & Easy Guide to American Sign Language*. New York: Sterling, 2004.

McCully, Emily Arnold. *My Heart Glow: Alice Cogswell, Thomas Gallaudet and the Birth of American Sign Language*. New York: Hyperion, 2008.

Schaefer, Lola M. *Some Kids Are Deaf*. Mankato, Minn: Capstone Press, 2008.

Internet Addresses

KidsHealth: What's Hearing Loss?
<http://kidshealth.org/kid/health_problems/sight/hearing_impairment.html>

"The Legacy Begins"—Gallaudet University
<http://www.gallaudet.edu/x229.xml>

"Sign Design"—PBS Kids
<http://pbskids.org/arthur/print/signdesign/index.html>

Index